GW01458385

Handwriting
6–7

Author: Stephanie Cooper
Illustrator: Emma Holt and Chris McGhie

Letts

How to use this book

Look out for these features!

Parents

IN THE ACTIVITIES

The parents' notes at the top of each activity will give you:
► a simple explanation about what your child is learning
► an idea of how you can work with your child on the activity.

44

This small page number guides you to the back of the book, where you will find further ideas for help.

AT THE BACK OF THE BOOK

Every activity has a section for parents containing:
► further explanations about what the activity teaches
► games that can be easily recreated at home
► questions to ask your child to encourage their learning
► tips on varying the activity if it seems too easy or too difficult for your child.

You will also find the answers at the back of the book.

HELPING YOUR CHILD AS THEY USE THIS BOOK

Why not try starting at the beginning of the book and work through it? Your child should only attempt one activity at a time. Remember, it is best to learn little and often when we are feeling wide awake!

EQUIPMENT YOUR CHILD WILL NEED

► a pencil for writing
► an eraser for correcting mistakes
► coloured pencils for drawing and colouring in.

You might also like to have ready some spare paper and some collections of objects (for instance, small toys, Lego bricks, buttons...) for some of the activities.

Contents

Short oo words 4

ar words 6

oy words 8

ow words 10

air words 12

or words 14

er words 16

ear words 18

ea words 20

Sound families 22

More sound families 24

Sort out the sounds 26

Work out the words 28

Joined-up handwriting 30

Join the letters 32

More handwriting joins 34

Joining short to tall 36

More short and tall 38

Joining tall letters 40

Joining tail letters 42

Further activities 44

Celebration! 48

Short oo words

Write these words. As you write, say each
word aloud and listen to the **oo** sound.

pull _____   wool _____

bull _____   shook _____

put _____   hook _____

push _____   took _____

good _____   book _____

Percy Pull and Peter
Push the farmers wanted
to put Fred the bull in
the shed.

Percy pulled and Peter
pushed, but Fred just
stood still.

This activity will help your child to learn how to write and spell words with the short 'oo', as in 'book'.

Ask them to use the words on page 4 to help them finish the story.

Parents

44

They shook and shook Fred. "This is no good," said Percy. "Take a good look, he hasn't moved."

Now draw a picture and finish writing the story.

ar words

Write these words. As you write, say each word aloud and listen to the **ar** sound.

are _____   shark _____

car _____   star _____

bark _____   start _____

garden _____   park _____

market _____   dark _____

Can you find any more **ar** words in the pictures?
List them on some spare paper.

➤ This activity will help your child to learn how to write and spell correctly words with the 'ar' sound.

➤ Begin by highlighting the 'ar' letters with your child first.

Parents

44

BEWARE SHARKS

LARGE CAR PARK

START

Barley's Supermarket

3 for the price of 2!

Special offer!

Fun Tonight

Frankie Starr in 1 man and his guitar!

oy words

Write these words. As you write, say each word aloud and listen to the **oy** sound.

oy! _____   soil _____

oi! _____   boy _____

toy _____   Roy _____

oil _____   royal _____

foil _____   spoil _____

Can you find any more **oy** words in the picture? List them here.

_____

Parents

This activity will help your child to learn how to write and spell correctly words with the 'oy' sound.

Make sure they understand the meaning of the 'oy' words on the page.

44

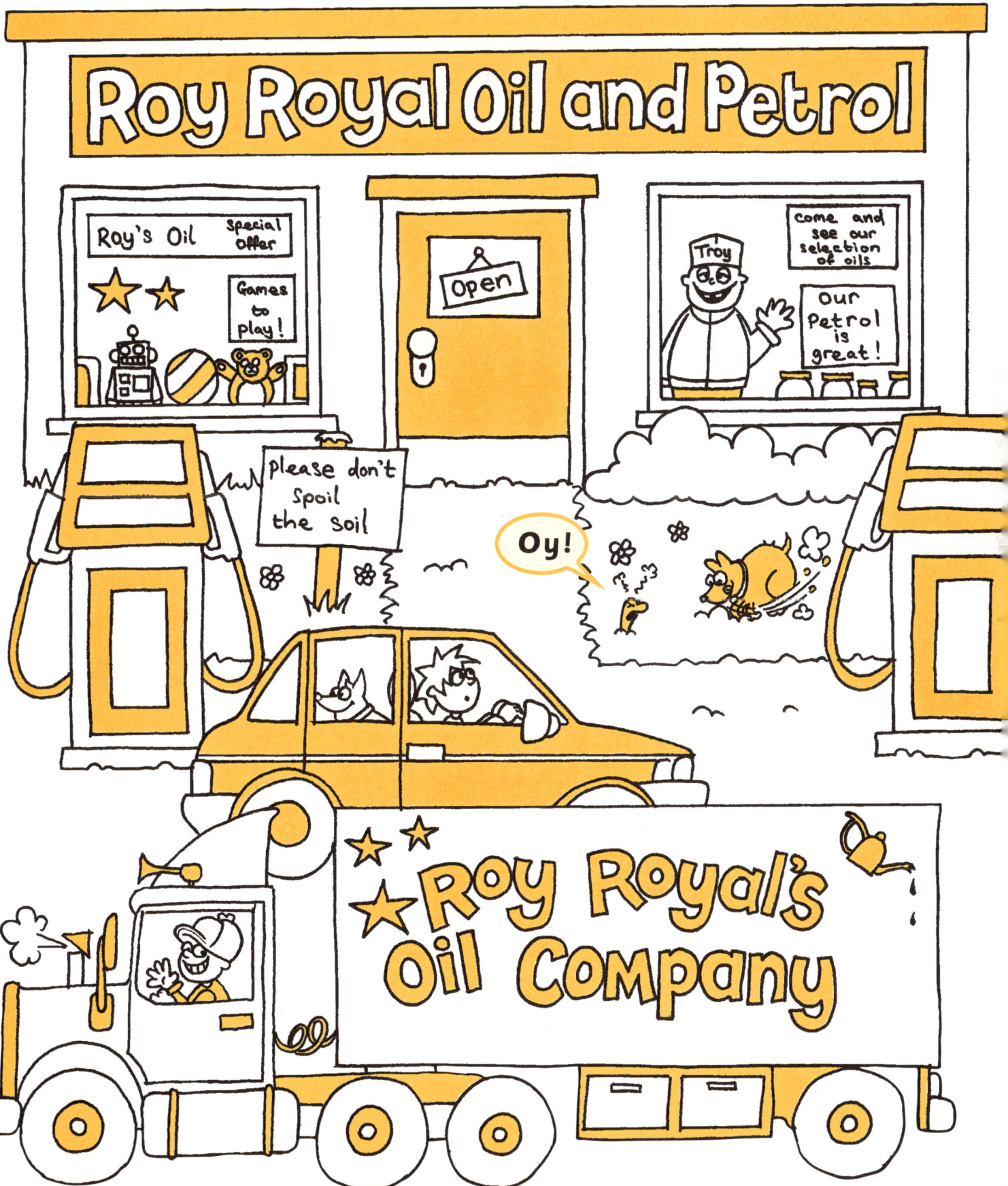

ow words

Write these words with the **ow** sound.
Then look for more in the pictures.

ow! _____   down _____

bough _____   about _____

how _____   hour _____

now _____   mouth _____

pow _____   ground _____

_____

_____

A new crown will cost
a thousand pounds.

This activity will help your child to learn how to write and spell correctly words with the 'ow' sound.

First, ask them to draw a circle around the 'ow' sounds in each word.

I've found a round house.

Roundtown

FOR SALE

Wow, a brown cow!

I'm shouting as loud as I can!

air words

Write these words.

air _____   ere _____

are _____   ear _____

What shall we wear today?

Where is my hairbrush?

Now look for the **air** words in these pictures. List them here.

_____

_____

_____

► This activity will help your child learn how to write and spell correctly words with the 'air' sound.

► Ask them to write the 'air' words they find in the pictures.

Parents

44

13

or words

Write these words with the **or** sound.
Then look for some more in the pictures.

or _____   shorts _____

awe _____   saw _____

ore _____   sport _____

door _____   draw _____

yawn _____   more _____

Ssh Claud. I'm trying to draw.

Yawn!

This train is going North to York.

More tea or coffee?

▶ This activity will help your child to learn how to write and spell correctly words with the 'or' sound.

▶ Ask them to draw a circle around each 'or' sound first.

Sports Hall

door

DORA

FLOR

List your words here.

_____

_____

er words

Write these sounds and words.

er _____   river _____

ir _____   bird _____

ur _____   rockery _____

fur _____   bird feeder _____

sunflowers _____   spider _____

Now draw some of these **er** sound words
in the picture.

butterflies

ladybirds

blackbirds

grasshoppers

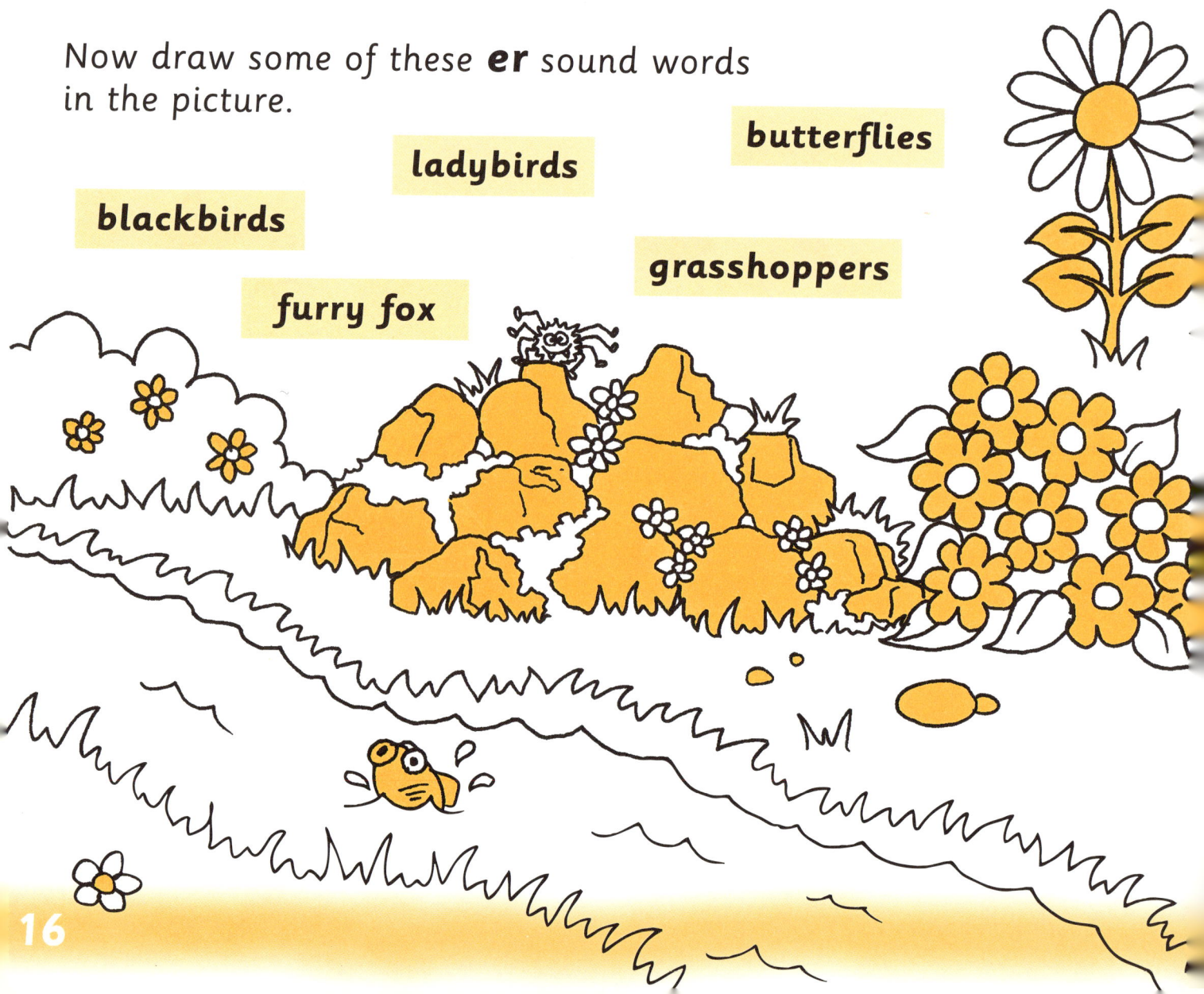

furry fox

16

This activity will help your child to learn how to write and spell correctly words with the 'er' sound.

Ask them to circle each 'er' sound in each word first.

ear words

Write these words.

ear _____   year _____

beard _____   hear _____

tear _____   fear _____

near _____   dear _____

Now add the **ear**-sound words in the picture.

_____

_____

18

This activity will help your child to learn how to write and spell correctly words with the 'ear' sound.

Point out that the word 'tear' can be said in two ways, and can mean two different things.

Stay near me, dear.

Coming next year — more rides!

Candy floss

HOOK THE DUCK

ea words

Write these sounds and words that rhyme with **bread**.
What do they all have in common?

ea _____   instead _____

bread _____   ready _____

head _____   tread _____

thread _____

Now write a sentence with the words you have just practised.

_____

_____

_____

_____

This activity will help your child to learn how to write and spell correctly words with the 'ea' sound.

Ask your child to use the pictures for ideas to help them write their own sentence.

3

4

_____

_____

_____

5 Ready, steady...

6

_____

_____

_____

Sound families

Look at these words carefully, then write each one inside the correct 'sound' balloon.

Flora

star

mouse

cow

fairy

bull

cloud

shark

square

bear

Dora

wool

clown

car

hair

book

stairs

arm

This activity will help your child learn how to write and spell correctly words with the short 'oo' sound, 'ow', 'ar', 'or' and 'air' sounds.

First, draw a circle around the letter clusters in each word.

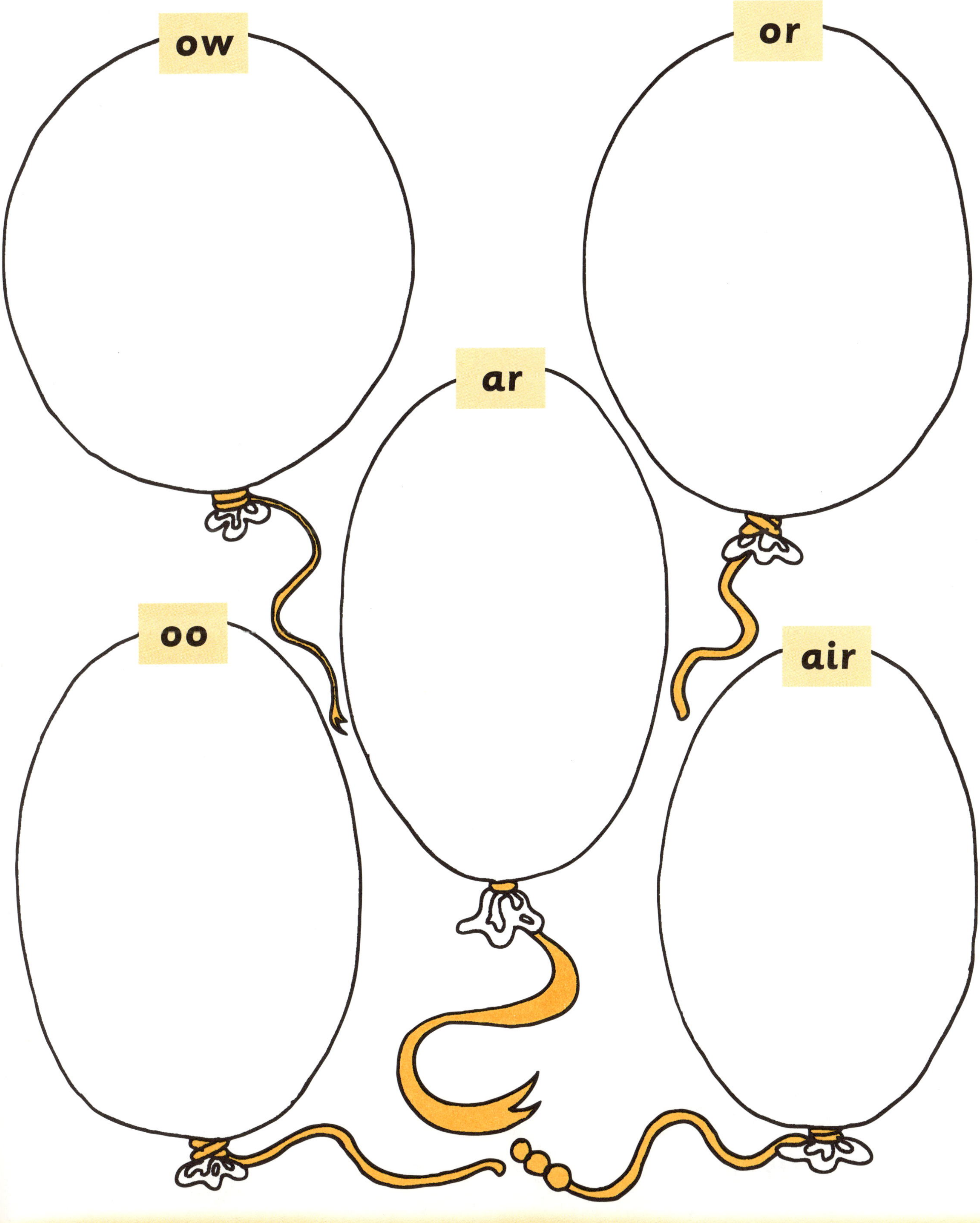

ow

or

ar

oo

air

More sound families

Look at these words carefully, then write each one inside the correct 'sound' balloon.

beard

ears

toaster

flower

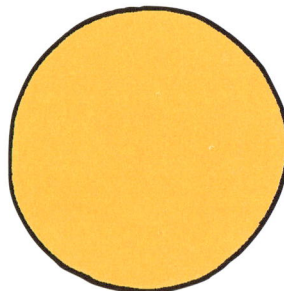

circle

head

boy

toy

bread

tiger

oil

24

This activity will help your child learn how to write and spell correctly, words with the 'er', 'ea', 'oy' and 'ear' sounds.

First, draw a circle around the letter clusters in each word.

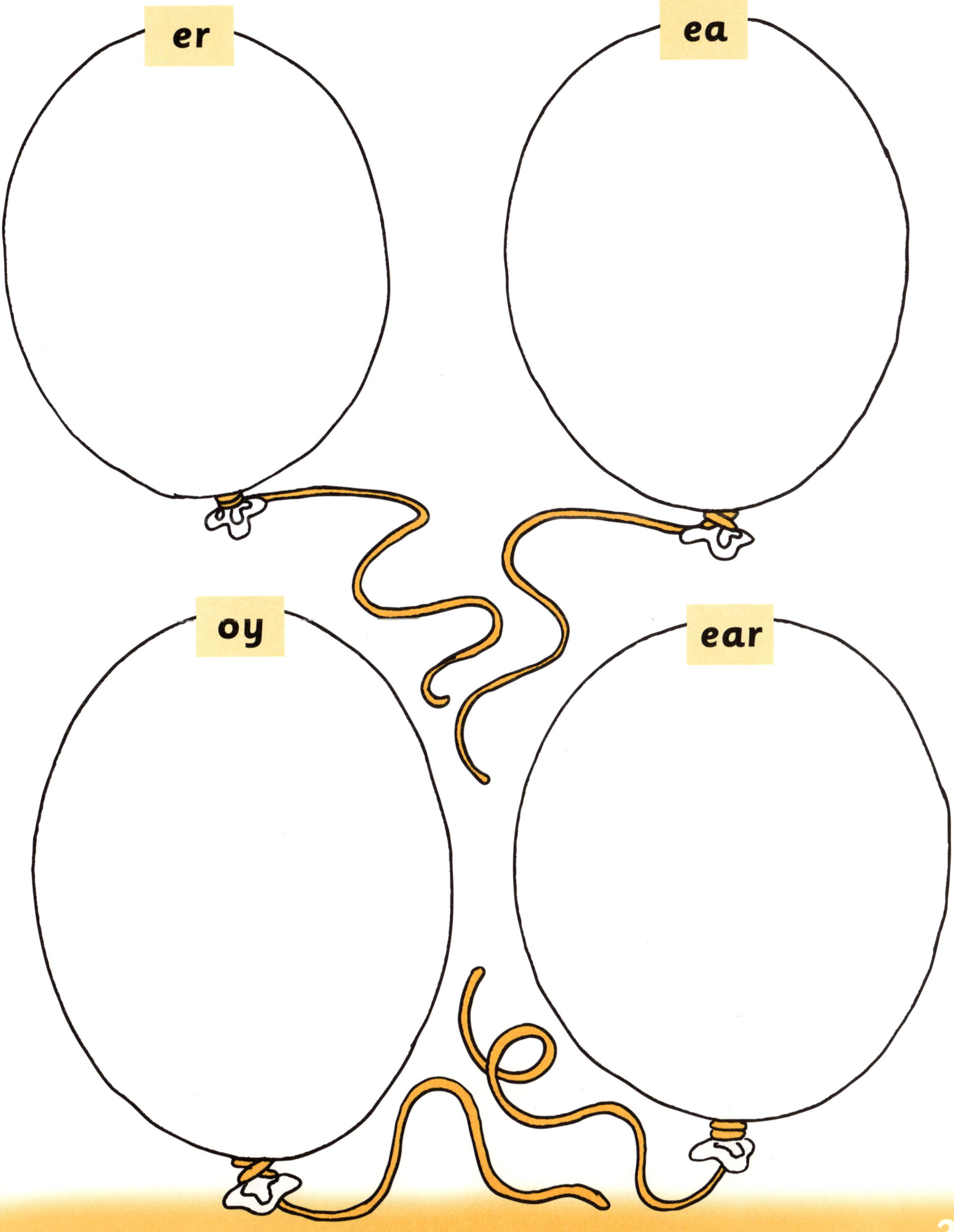

er

ea

oy

ear

Sort out the sounds

Circle the **er**, **ear**, **air** and **ar** sound words in the sentences below. Then write some silly sentences of your own.

1. Did you hear about the grocer who drew cabbages on his computer?

2. Did you hear about the monster with the beard and the sticky-out ears who burst into tears?

Parents

46

► This activity will help your child to learn how to write correctly words with the 'er', 'ear', 'air' and 'ar' sounds.

► Ask your child which sentence has the most 'er' words.

3. Did you hear about the bear and the fairy who did a square dance around a chair, then ate a pear?

4. Did you hear about the man with the scar who drove his car in the dark under the stars to see a shark far away?

Work out the words

pair

tear

caught

claw

store

fork

Look at the pictures in the border, and write each word in the correct 'sound' balloon.

ar

oo, u

er, ir, or, ur

car

wood

pull

28

► This activity will help your child to learn how to write and spell correctly words with 'ar', short 'oo' (u), 'er' (ir, or, ur), 'ow' (ou), 'air' (are, ere, ear) and 'or' (aw, au, ore) sounds.

ow, ou

air, are, ere, ear   **or, aw, au, ore**

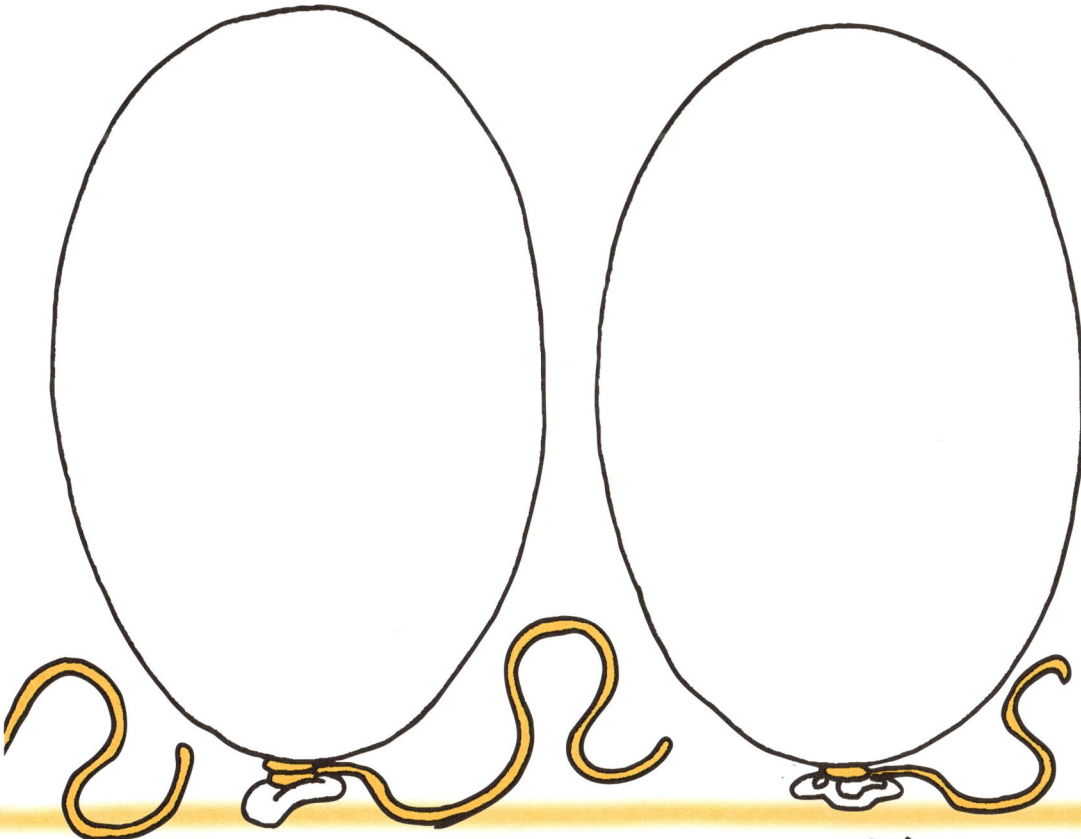

skirt

circle

shower

mouth

pear

nurse

purse

hare

Joined-up handwriting

Write the alphabet, then choose the tall, short and tail letters.

a b c d e f g h i j k l m

n o p q r s t u v w x y z

f

r

c

S

a

b

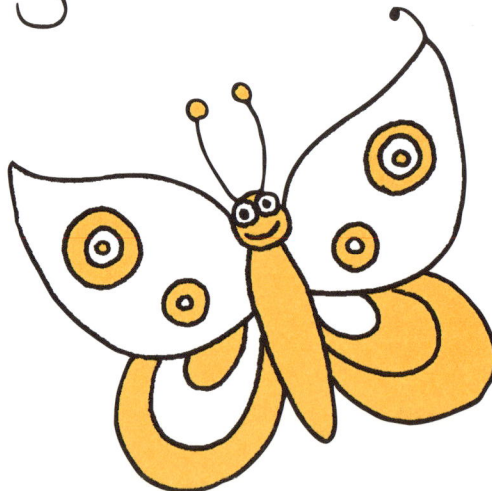

u

t

▶ This activity will help your child to learn how to write letters in a cursive style.

▶ Make sure they begin at the dot on each letter.

tall letters:

_____

short letters:

_____

letters with tails:

_____

Join the letters

must

man

Join these letters together, then practise writing some joined-up words of your own.

ng ——————— mu ———————

ue ——————— ur ———————

ne ——————— ni ———————

us ——————— ee ———————

———————————————

———————————————

make

name

been   Saturday   June

made    may

mum    January   Sunday

32

▶ This activity will help your child to learn how to join letters 'm', 'n', 'r', 's', 'u', 'e', 'a' and 'i'.

▶ When they are trying to write the words, focus on them being able to join these letters only, to avoid confusion.

na _____   mu _____

ue _____   ur _____

ne _____   ni _____

us _____   ee _____

_____

_____

_____

many

green

next

much

seen

Monday

Tuesday

Wednesday

more

am

More handwriting joins

there

very

want

come

Practise joining up these letters.
Then try writing some words of your own.

ou _____   vi _____

wi _____   on _____

or _____   wn _____

_____

_____

_____

down

about

 some

'one

Thursday

way

out

house

This activity will help your child learn how to write joins from 'o', 'v', 'w' and 'r' to the short letters in the alphabet.

Focus on these joins only when they are writing out the words.

om _____   oo _____

ve _____   wa _____

re _____   rs _____

ri _____

_____

_____

_____

were

home

door

from

our

too

should

where

over

Friday

Joining short to tall

about

went

must

cat

Join these letters together. Write some joined-up words of your own.

ab _____   ul _____

it _____   at _____

nt _____   al _____

sh _____   ak _____

_____

_____

call

make

out

not

February

July

water

December

This activity will help your child to learn how to join the letters 'a', 'u', 'i', 'c', 'e', 'm', 'n' and 's' to the tall letters 'h', 'k', 'l', 't' and 'b'.

Do correct them if they don't join the letters correctly.

ut _____   ch _____

st _____   il _____

mb _____   eb _____

nk _____

_____

_____

_____

make

sister

want

will

all

March

September

much

November

it

pink

37

More short and tall

look

got

Practise joining up these letters. Then try writing some words of your own.

ol _____   wh _____

ot _____   ok _____

who _____

_____

_____

_____

another

not

brother

38

This activity will help your child to learn how to join up the letters 'o' and 'w' to tall letters.

Encourage your child to join the letters in the right way – it will speed up their writing in the future.

what _____

when _____

where _____

_____

_____

_____

_____

school

October

white

look

39

Joining tall letters

black

blue

this

Practise joining up these tall letters.
Then join up some words of your own.

bl _____

th _____

_____

_____

_____

_____

they

these

called

all

ball

that

another

the

with

This activity will help your child to learn how to join up tall letters which they can then use in writing independently.

Make sure they write the tall letters taller than the short letters.

ll _____

ld _____

tt _____

_____

_____

_____

_____

could

than

three

them

will

then

should

little

there

old

their

41

Joining tail letters

orange

after

push

jump

Practise joining up these letters, then try writing some words of your own.

gr_____   ge_____

gu_____   pr_____

fo_____   go_____

yo_____   ye_____

_____

_____

yellow

put

you

got

good

girl

get

yes

zoo

42

This activity will help your child to learn how to join tail letters to short and tall letters.

Make sure they are able to write each join without removing their pencil from the page.

people

gi _____   ju _____

gh _____   pe _____

pl _____   pu _____

ft _____   zoo _____

_____

_____

_____

just

might

August

play

going

for

April

green

pull

your

Further activities

4-5

- Ask your child to practise writing other short 'oo' words, for example, 'full', 'wood' and 'look'.

- Talk about the difference between long 'oo' words (moon) and short 'oo' words (good).

- Introduce the letters 'oo' and 'u' written in a cursive style.

6-7

- Encourage your child to practise writing other 'ar' words, for example, 'are', 'tart' and 'star', and to look for more in story and reference books. Introduce the letters 'ar' written in a cursive style.

- *Answers: go-kart, start, tar, car, far, Starr, guitar, gardens, bark, large car park, sharks, Barley's supermarket. Your child may find others.*

8-9

- Invite your child to make up their own 'oi' and 'oy' words, both real and imagined, to make sure they can say the sound correctly, for example, 'woil' or 'doy'.

- Then ask your child to look up other 'oy' and 'oi' words in a dictionary and to practise writing them.

Make sure they are writing each letter correctly, making tall letters tall, and putting tails on the tail letters.

- *Answers: Roy, Royal, oil, foil, soil, oy, spoil, toys, Troy. Your child may find others.*

10-11

- Help your child to practise writing the 'ow' words they have found.

- To develop this, ask them to write a tongue twister using mainly 'ow' words, for example, 'How now brown cow' or 'There's a clown with a brown crown in town'.

- *Answers: crown, counter, thousand, pounds round, house, Roundtown, found wow, brown, cow ground, shouting, loud. Your child may find others.*

12-13

- Ask your child to make a list of other 'air' words, including 'air', 'hare', 'scare', 'share', 'care' and 'tear', which they can then use in independent writing.

- Regularly ask them to highlight the 'air' sound in each word, so that they learn that the sound is made by joining three letters together.

- *Answers: 'wear', 'where', 'hairbrush', 'there', 'bear', 'fair hair', 'stare'. There may be some others.*

► Make a list of other 'or' words, including 'for', 'claw', 'dawn', 'fork' and 'store'.

► To extend this activity further, introduce your child to 'caught' and 'taught', which are both 'or' words. Then show them how to write these words in a cursive style.

► *Answers: Claud, York, yawn, draw, North, more, or, Dora, Flora, sports, shorts, door. Your child may find others.*

► Ask your child to practise writing more 'er' words, such as 'her', 'were', 'after', 'other' and 'circle' which they will then be able to use when they write independently.

► Also introduce them to less common words, such as 'butter', 'purse', 'shirt', 'paper' and 'danger'.

► To broaden their experience, ask them to write a sentence about each new word they learn or just talk about what each word means. How would they use the word 'danger', for example?

► Point out the difference in spelling and meaning between the words 'hear' and 'here'. Also point out the difference between 'hear' and 'pear', which both have 'ear' endings but which are pronounced differently.

► Ask your child to write a list of words that rhyme with 'tear' ('wear', 'bear', 'pear') and then words that rhyme with 'hear' ('dear', 'gear', 'year').

► *Answers: near, dear, fear, year, here. Your child may find others.*

► With your child, make a list of 'ea' words, then ask them to think of more words that rhyme with 'head' and 'bread'. Point out that 'red', 'bed' and 'ted' words all make the same sound without the 'ea' blend in the middle.

► Point out the difference in pronounciation between 'neat' and 'head', which both have the same 'ea' letters.

► Revise each sound family with your child as often as you can. Spend time practising how to write 'ow' words, for example, then look for 'ow' words in a story or reference book.

► Talk about how the words sound and how they look. Repeat this for each word family.

► *Answers: 'ow' words: clown, cloud, mouse, cow; short 'oo' words: bull, wool, book; 'ar' words: arm, shark, car, star; 'or' words: Dora, Flora; 'air' words: hair, fairy, bear, stairs, square.*

45

Further activities

24-25

▶ Simplify this activity, if necessary, by splitting each word into its component parts, and writing them down on a piece of paper. For example, c/ir/cle, toa/st/er, ti/g/er. This will help your child to see each part clearly.

These letter groups are known as phonemes – a word your child may be familiar with. Repeat this for each word family, one at a time.

▶ *Answers: 'er' words: circle, toaster, tiger, flower; 'ea' words: bread, head; 'oy' words: boy, toy, oil; 'ear' words: beard, ears.*

26-27

▶ Ask your child which sentence has the most 'ear' sound words (2), which sentence has the most 'air' sound words (3) and which sentence has the most 'ar' sound words (4).

▶ To extend this further, write another sentence for them to identify the 'er' words, for example, 'Did you hear about the nurse who put a furry fox in her purse?'

▶ *Answers: 'er' sound words: grocer, computer, monster; 'ear' sound words: hear, beard, ears, tears; 'air' sound words: bear, fairy, square, chair, pear; 'ar' sound words: scar, car, dark, stars, shark, far.*

28-29

▶ Help your child to write other words in each balloon by looking back through the book for ideas. Write all the new words they have learned into a word book, with all the words in alphabetical order so that they can look up words on their own.

▶ Encourage your child to write some words that you dictate to them such as 'nurse', 'purse', 'fur', one day, then 'bird', 'shirt', 'skirt', the next, and so on.

▶ *Answers: 'ar' sound word: car; short 'oo' sound words: wood, pull; 'er' sound words: nurse, purse, circle, skirt; 'ow' sound words: mouth, shower; 'air' sound words: pear, hare, pair, tear; 'or' sound words: caught, claw, store, fork.*

30-31

▶ Talk with your child about how the letters look different, and how to write them with an entry stroke at the beginning and a flick at the end.

▶ Point out that they need to start writing each letter in a different place, and that some letters, like 'k' and 'z', look completely different.

▶ *Answers: tall letters: b, d, h, k, l, t; short letters: a, c, e, i, m, n, o, r, s, u, v, w, x; tail letters: f, g, j, p, q, y, z.*

32-33

▶ Before your child starts handwriting practice, ask them to do a few exercises to loosen up their hands.

Ask them to wiggle their fingers and thumbs, one at a time, then to stretch all their fingers as far as they can. Then to turn each hand around in a circle from their wrist. Ask them to shake their hands, and to pretend they are trying to 'throw away' their fingers. Then to move their shoulders in a circle. Finally, to stretch their arms up above their head and stretch. This will loosen them up for handwriting.

► For more practice joining these letters together, ask your child to trace over your own writing, then to try on their own.

Think of other familiar words with these joins in that your child can try – their name, address, the name and address of their school.

► Write some words for them so they can continue to read joined-up writing.

► Have fun with your child by 'sky-writing' each join before writing on paper.

► Then write with a variety of pens, pencils, felt tips, crayons, chalks, charcoal and paint to make a coloured alphabet. Ask them to make the tall letters as tall as they can, or as thin as they can.

► To extend this further, introduce the number words to twenty with tall letters (such as, three, eight, thirteen, eighteen).

► Suggest that your child writes these letters by gluing a piece of string onto paper, making sure that the join is correct.

► Let them practise with pencils and pens on lined and non-lined paper, in a variety of colours.

► Introduce them to other words with these joins and to names of people they know, as well as common words ('hot' and 'while') which they can then use in their own writing.

► Ask your child to write the days of the week.

► Give them words with letters missing which they have to write in for example, wa_ _, (wall) fa_ _, (fall) li_ _le (little).

► Write some letter clusters upside down, and on their side, and ask them to write them correctly the right way up.

► Make a wall poster with your child by writing the 12 months of the year in joined-up writing, and decorated with common colour words (black, blue, orange, brown, red, pink, yellow, white, green).

► Show them how to write and spell the numbers 'one', 'two', 'three' 'four', 'five', 'six', 'seven',

'eight', 'nine', 'ten', 'eleven', 'twelve' and 'thirteen', and all the other numbers up to nineteen.

Celebration!

You are so clever! Colour the stars to show what you can do!

I can write five 'oo' words.

I can write five 'ar' words.

I can write five 'ow' words.

I can do joined-up handwriting.